A MODERN APPROACH TO CLASSICAL GUITAR

Book Two

By CHARLES DUNCAN

W9-BMP-545

CONTENTS

HAL•LEONARD®
CORPORATION

7777 W. BLUEMOUND RD. P.O. BOX 13819 MILWAUKEE, WI 53213

TO THE PLAYER

To progress through the material ahead, you need to have mastered the skills covered in Book One. Specifically, these are:

- Tuning the guitar.

- Playing alternating i - m rest-stroke.

- Playing fingers and thumb together.

- Recognizing all the notes in the first position.

- Recognizing various basic musical time indications.

- Playing Am, E, and Dm chords with bass-brush strum.

The lessons ahead contain new techniques for both the right and left hands. Also, you will learn notes on the fingerboard as far as the 6th fret and will become acquainted with the classical guitar solo repertoire. As in Book One, there are many student-teacher duets. **This book is available as a book/CD and "book only" version.** The teacher's part is included on the CD so you can practice your part together with the teacher's; look for the ◆ symbol in the margin. A tuning track is included as track 1 of the CD.

Try to increase your practice time to an hour a day during the coming months. As in the development of any physical skill, results are proportional to effort. How you practice is just as important as how much. Practice all new material very slowly and carefully. Even when a piece is to be played fast, practice very slowly when learning and you will be rewarded by rapid progress.

THE FREE-STROKE WITH THE FINGERS

Whenever more than two notes are played at the same time, the **free-stroke** is used. It is also used when notes are played on adjacent strings, either together or consecutively. Three or more notes played simultaneously are referred to as **chords.** A consecutive pattern of notes played on adjacent strings is known as an **arpeggio** (from Italian **arpa**, meaning "harp").

Arpeggio and chord playing require use of the ring finger of the right hand. The ring finger is designated by a letter **a** (for Spanish **anular).**

The wrist position for free stroke is a little higher than for rest stroke—3-4 inches from the top of the guitar when the thumb and fingers are placed on the strings, as shown below:

Avoid flattening the knuckles. When positioned correctly, the fingers should escape the next lower string on a very shallow angle.

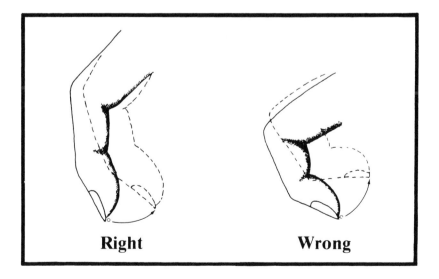

Right   **Wrong**

You can use a Ping-Pong ball to help learn a good free-stroke hand position. Simply grasp the ball in the palm of the hand, then place your fingers on the strings. The ball will automatically form your hand into a correct position. (If you don't have a Ping-Pong ball, a wadded-up piece of paper will do.)

FILING THE FINGERNAILS

This section and the next are for those students whose nails are in basically good shape and who would like to learn to use them correctly. If for one reason or another you cannot begin using your fingernails at this time, treat these two sections as a reference guide to be returned to later.

The shape of the nail should **not** be long and pointed, but relatively short and blunt. The nail should project about 1/16 inch beyond the fingertip (1/8 inch for the thumb) seen from underneath.

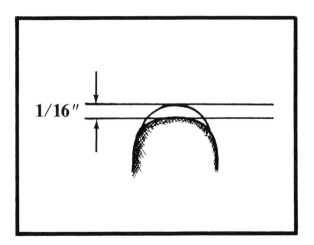

The **exact** shape the nail takes when properly filed, seen from underneath, will differ from person to person, and even from one finger to another on the same hand. This is because of variance in the arch-contour of nails. (Look at your fingertips head-on to see the arch-contour of the nails.) Not all nails have the highest point of the arch in the center. Some have it on the right; some have it on the left. Still others turn down in the center. No matter where the highest point of the arch-contour is as seen head on, it should be the longest point of the nail when seen from underneath. In the case of a nail that turns down in the center, the nail should have a squared-off appearance seen from underneath when correctly filed.

For detailed discussion and illustrations of the various nail types, see the author's **The Art Of Classical Guitar Playing** (Princeton, NJ: Summy-Birchard Music, 1980) Chapter 4.

Learning to file your nails to just the right shape will take patience. Here are some general points to guide you:

Use a metal file that has a blade covered with industrial gemstone (tradenames such as Diamon Deb, Diama-file, etc.). Hold the file at about a 45° angle to the nail. Use short back-and-forth strokes.

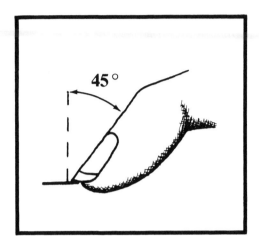

File with the nail just a little below eye level so that your view of the nail is as below:

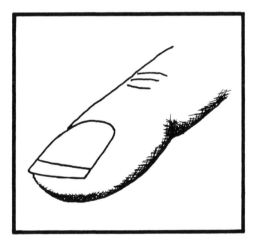

Try to shape the nail so that its edge appears as a shallow curve, or even a straight line, as in the illustration. Avoid any kind of dip, wiggle, notch, etc. in the line of the edge.

Finish the nail with a very fine grade of abrasive paper. Number 600 emery paper will do a good job; so will crocus cloth. Both are available at large hardware stores. "Jewelers' paper" (4/0 polishing paper) is favored by many advanced players for an absolutely nick-free final finish, but is a little harder to find. (Craft shops that include jewelry-making supplies usually have it; so do many guitar shops.) No matter what paper you use, the objective is a slick, glossy edge to the nail that will pass over the string without a snag.

USING THE NAILS

For all strokes, the string should make simultaneous contact with the nail and the tip of the finger. The flesh of the fingertip does not actually engage the string—instead it damps the string from above. The sound is produced by the nail alone.

For the **i**, **m**, and **a** fingers, the nail engages the string at one point on the left side (the side nearest the thumb). In playing, the nail will thus glide across the string from left to right.

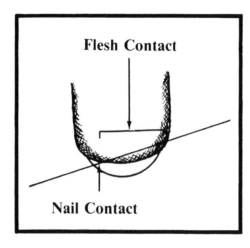

Flesh Contact

Nail Contact

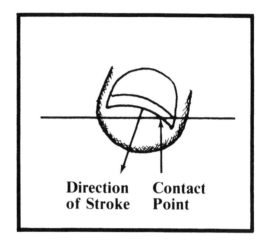

Direction of Stroke   **Contact Point**

The exact amount of angle varies, but a completely perpendicular attack is used only for an intentionally brittle or glassy tone.

In the case of the thumb, the nail-to-string contact point for most players is near the **center** of the nail.

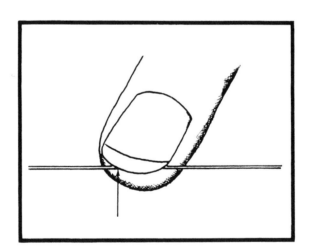

As the thumb plays, the string glides along the edge of the nail and releases near the down side corner.

BEGINNING FREE-STROKE
EXERCISES

You can get the feel of the free-stroke by playing **i**, **m**, and **a** in the following patterns on the open treble strings. (If you are not yet using fingernails, simply use the tips of your fingers.) Rest your thumb on the 6th string for support.

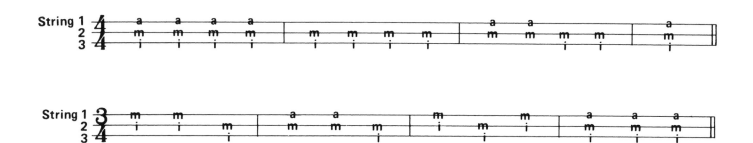

Playing a good free-stroke isn't entirely a matter of plucking upward. Actually, it's more of a down-and-in push followed by a release. TIP: It's like notching, drawing, and releasing an arrow—the ''arrow'' being the actual sound. Listen carefully to the tone quality. When you can produce clear, simultaneous-sounding chords, go on to the following exercises.

Fold Hand thumb anchored

Use **m** and **i**

A dash before a number (-2) indicates that the finger should **remain held down** from the previous fingering.

Use **a**, **m** and **i**

THE THUMB AND FINGERS TOGETHER

The thumb is generally used to play the lowest note of all chords, regardless of whether the chords have two, three or four notes.

The following exercise is similar to the type of exercises you played in the last few lessons of Book One, but with an important difference: here both the fingers and the thumb are playing the free-stroke. Be sure that the fingers play the free-stroke, **not** the rest-stroke.

Three-note chords are usually played with the thumb, index and middle fingers. Remember to push down and in at the beginning of each chord; let the actual sound come from a release, not an upward pluck. Observe left-hand fingering carefully.

ARPEGGIOS WITH p-i-m

An arpeggio can be thought of as a broken chord. Place your fingers on the strings at the beginning of each measure as if you were going to play a single chord; then, play each finger in turn. This will greatly aid in developing right-hand security.

In the next exercise, notice the dashes that indicate the 2nd finger is serving as a **pivot** finger. (A pivot finger remains held down while other fingers move.) Notice also that the first note in each measure is a dotted half; it continues to ring while the second and third notes are played.

The next exercise, **p-i-m-i,** adds a note to the previous pattern. Once again, the first note in each measure functions as a bass note for the entire measure. The Double stem, which indicates this, is common in arpeggios. Let all notes ring until the chord changes.

CHORD CONSTRUCTION

Before progressing further in technique, you should become acquainted with the theory of chord construction.

The most common type of scale is called **diatonic** (from Greek **diatonos**, "at the interval of a tone"). Such scales contain **seven** different intervals counting upward from the first note.

The interval between tone one and two is a second, from one to three a third, from one to four a fourth, etc.

You can also start with a note other than the key note and determine intervals. Call that note one, then count up or down (alternating line/space, space/line) to find the interval.

Certain harmonic intervals such as thirds and sixths automatically sound good. These intervals are known as **consonant** intervals; you will see them frequently in the music you play.

Stacked thirds are the basis of most chords. Two stacked thirds produce a **triad**, named for its **root** or bottom note. The interval from the root to the upper note is a fifth.

Any of the three basic triad tones can be doubled at the octave to make the chord sound fuller. Most common guitar chords involve doubling one or more of the basic triad tones.

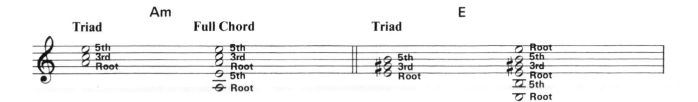

Major and **minor** are chord qualities determined by the first interval of the basic triad. The third (middle note) of the minor triad is one-half step lower than the third of a major triad.

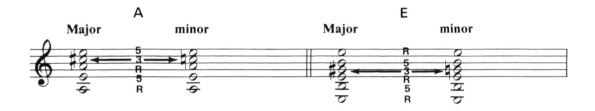

When three thirds are stacked, the interval from the root to the highest note is a seventh.

Such chords are called seventh chords. Because of the tuning of the guitar, they seldom appear in the closed voicing shown above. Usually they appear in a more open voicing, as shown below.

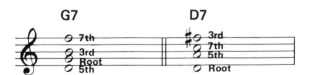

CHORDS AND FOUR-NOTE ARPEGGIOS

To play four-note chords and arpeggios, the fingers **p-i-m-a** are used. In the following exercise, the **a** finger carries the melody. Can you hear it clearly? Be sure the **a** finger plays with the same force as the other fingers. TIP: It helps to compress the fingers together, starting from the little finger. The more compact the hand, the more solid the stroke of the **a** finger.

Note the key signature—all F's are sharped.

The most basic four-note arpeggio is the **p-i-m-a** movement. As in the case of the **p-i-m** arpeggio, treat this as a broken chord. Place the fingers on their strings at the beginning of each group of four notes. Be sure to observe the key signature too—all the 4th string F's are sharped.

REFLECTIONS

C. Duncan

12

Arpeggios can make attractive solo pieces, or they can serve as patterns for chordal accompaniment. One of the most useful arpeggios for either purpose is the 3/4 arpeggio, **p-i-m-a-m-i**. Here, it makes a simple but effective accompaniment to a well-known English traditional ballad. Use your thumb rest-stroke when playing the fifth or sixth string. Many players prefer to do so in this type of arpeggio.

SCARBOROUGH FAIR

FIRST CLASSICAL SOLOS

Ferdinand Carulli (1770-1841) was one of the most important composers of student-level guitar music. Besides being a virtuoso player himself, he was a teacher and had a special flair for composing short pieces that are easy, but sound good.

In the COUNTRY DANCE, as in most of his compositions, Carulli uses a very symmetrical periodic structure (**period** is the term for a complete musical thought consisting of eight bars). Each period is repeated, and within the first two there are clearly defined four-bar phrases. The third is somewhat less formal in design and is in a contrasting minor key. It serves as a kind of interlude before the return to the beginning, signalled by the words **D.C. al Fine**. D.C. stands for **Da Capo** ("from the beginning"); **al Fine** means "to the end." Whenever you see this, it means go back to the beginning and play up to the point marked "Fine," or end. Do not play repeats on the D.C. al Fine.

The right-hand technique of the piece is free-stroke throughout. The tempo marking, **Allegretto**, means moderately fast.

COUNTRY DANCE

Carulli

14

The WALTZ has similar stylistic features. As in the COUNTRY DANCE, the periods are constructed with an eye to internal symmetry and the melody is supported by a broken chordal harmony. The melody in this case is formed by the third and fifth notes of the arpeggio pattern in each measure. To make the melody clearly heard, accent the **a** and **m** fingers. Be sure to hold down the 4th finger when it plays a melody note until the next melody note is sounded. (That is, don't release it when you play the open-string G which follows it.) The tempo marking, **Allegro**, indicates that the music is to be played at a fast tempo once it is learned; try to make it sound like the lively dance indicated by the title.

WALTZ

Carulli

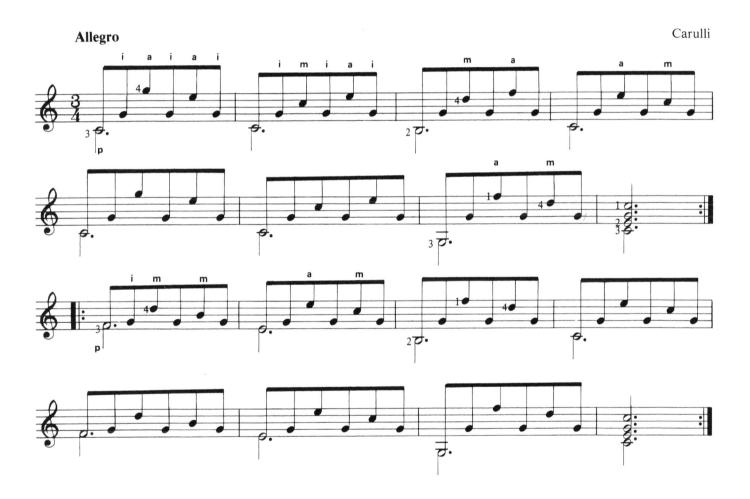

MORE ABOUT CHORDS

Chords may be constructed on all seven notes of any diatonic scale. The chords so constructed make up a family of key-related chords.

Of particular importance are the chords built on the first, fourth and fifth notes of the scale. They are known as the **primary chords** for that key and are called the **tonic**, **subdominant**, and **dominant**. The dominant is often a seventh chord.

In the key of A minor, you already know them:

In the key of C, the chords built on the first and fifth notes of the scale are C and G7:

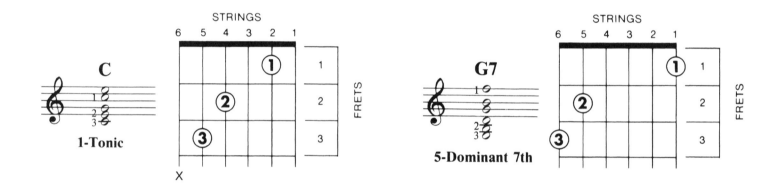

Note that the G7 is like an expanded C. Practice changing from C to G7 by leading with your third finger (**not** your first). This will make simultaneous movement of all the fingers come more quickly. Use the thumb brush-stroke (indicated by a wavy line) on the following exercise:

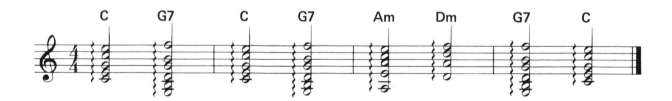

16

F MAJOR: THE BAR

The chord built on the fourth step of the C scale is F:

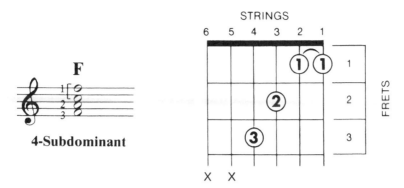

F

4-Subdominant

This chord introduces an important new left hand technique—**barring**. Bar chords are those in which the first finger depresses more than one string.

The bar required for the F chord is a half-bar (the half-bar consists of 2 or 3 strings). Although only two strings must be depressed, many players find it more comfortable to let the tip of the finger cover the third string as well. For this kind of bar, the first finger should appear as shown below:

Flatten your first finger from the middle joint to the tip as in the photograph above. The knuckle of the middle joint should be sharply bent so that it can exert leverage. Make sure that your thumb is well in back of the neck as shown. The thumb in all bar chords must oppose the first finger (like the jaws of a pair of pliers).

Practice the following chord changes (using the thumb brush-stroke) until all four notes of the F chord clearly sound before progressing further.

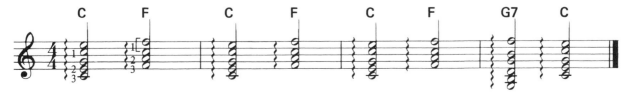

CHORDS AND ARPEGGIOS IN SONG ACCOMPANIMENT

The most widespread use of the guitar in all its forms is as an accompaniment for the voice. Classical guitar playing is essentially solo playing, but the skills developed also provide a basis for accompanying songs. You can have a lot of fun doing this, even if you yourself don't sing. For example, you might get together with another student who plays guitar (or recorder, flute, etc.). Using chords and arpeggios this way will also benefit your classical guitar technique.

One basic style of chordal accompanying is a refinement of the bass-brush technique covered in Book One. You play a bass note with the thumb, then play three treble notes together with the **a-m-i** fingers. In 3/4 time, the pattern is **thumb-fingers-fingers**:

In 4/4 time the pattern is **thumb-fingers-thumb-fingers**. Notice the alternation of bass notes for variety.

Arpeggios may also be used—especially when the melody is rather slow. The basic arpeggio pattern for 3/4 is **p-i-m-a-m-i**. For 4/4, it is **p-i-m-a, p-i-m-a**.

The following songs contain examples of each accompaniment style illustrated above. Practice each accompaniment (lower staff) as an exercise. When you can play it fluently, play along with the recorded melody. Play the melodies too for additional practice in sight reading.

AMAZING GRACE

SHALOM CHAVERIM

MICHAEL, ROW THE BOAT ASHORE

COCKLES AND MUSSELS illustrates the use of abbreviated chord fingerings, an important aspect of classical guitar technique. Since the arpeggio pattern does not require all the notes of the standard chord form (except for the Dm chord), you should finger only those notes that you will actually play. Omit the 2nd finger from the C and G7 chords, and substitute the 2nd for the 3rd finger in the Am chord. This will result in a much easier and more fluent movement from chord to chord.

COCKLES AND MUSSELS

$\frac{6}{8}$ TIME

Until now you have played time signatures in which the quarter note received one beat. In $\frac{6}{8}$ time the bottom number tells you that the eighth note now gets one beat. The top number means that there are six beats in one measure. Practice this new time signature in the following exercise. Use the **m-i** rest stroke.

IRISH WASHER WOMAN

In $\frac{6}{8}$ time all note and rest values are proportionate to the eighth note.

$\flat$ (♪)	$\downarrow$ (𝄾)	$\downarrow.$ (𝄼·)	$\downarrow.$ (—)
1 BEAT	**2 BEATS**	**3 BEATS**	**6 BEATS**

When $\frac{6}{8}$ is played at a faster tempo, there is a definite feel of 2 strong beats to the measure (beats 1 and 4). You can think of the beat unit in faster $\frac{6}{8}$ time as the dotted quarter note. Try tapping your foot on beats 1 and 4.

A-HUNTING WE WILL GO

Notice that the accompaniment to this famous American Civil War ballad is in dotted quarter notes, corresponding to the strong beats of the measure (1 and 4). Notice also in the next to the last measure the use of all open strings to harmonize the melody.

WHEN JOHNNY COMES MARCHING HOME

ACCENTING THE MELODY IN ARPEGGIOS

In the Carulli WALTZ (p. 15) you saw how a melody was part of an arpeggio. In many such pieces, the melody must be played with a rest-stroke for proper emphasis. When this is the case, the **a** finger usually plays a rest-stroke on the first string; the **m** finger plays a rest-stroke on the second string; while the **i** finger plays a **free-stroke** on the third string. In order to accustom the fingers to this new task, practice the following exercise using the rest-stroke with the **a** and **m** fingers:

Like Carulli, Matteo Carcassi (1792-1853) composed many fine student-level pieces. The title ANDANTINO is a tempo marking that is a little slower than allegretto. (Be sure that **i** plays free-stroke! If you fall into an unconscious rest-stroke with **i**, then the relationship between melody and harmony will become confused.) In the second line of the piece, the melody and harmony are on adjacent strings. Here, of course, the rest-stroke is not possible. The **i-m** fingers play together with a free-stroke.

ANDANTINO

Carcassi

Mauro Giuliani (1781-1839) was one of the finest guitarists and guitar composers of the 19th century. Many of his compositions can be heard today in concerts and on recordings.

MODERATO is constructed of a slow lyrical melody and a rippling arpeggio figure in the bass. Use the rest-stroke only on the dotted quarter notes in the melody. Everything else (including the eighth-notes of the melody line) is to be played with a free-stroke. Combining rest and free strokes this way is common among good players.

This piece contains some left-hand difficulties in the first two measures of lines two and four. Be prepared to spend some extra time on these passages to bring them up to fluency.

MODERATO

Giuliani

MUSIC THEORY REVIEW

1. Identify the interval from the lower to the higher note (count line-space-line, using 1 for the first note).

Interval: 4th _____ _____ _____ _____ _____ _____ _____

2. The following intervals are _____ .

3. The abbreviation D.C. stands for _____ _____ and tells

   you to _____ .

4. Write the name of each chord above the chord:

5. A period consists of _____ measures.

6. The Italian word, **fine**, means _____ .

7. Write in the correct time signature.

PLAYING BEYOND THE FIRST POSITION

In tuning the guitar, you learned that the sound of the open 5th string was the same as the 6th string at the fifth fret, the open 4th string the same as the 5th string at the fifth fret, and so on.

This pattern of repetition is known as the **rule of five frets**. Any note is found again on the next lower-pitched string five frets higher. The only exception is second string notes, which are always found again **four** frets higher on the third string. For example, the notes B and F may be played in the positions shown below.

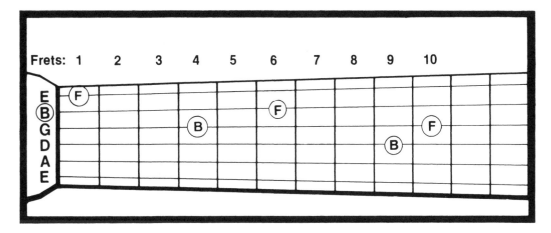

Moving notes to different places on the neck is called **position playing**. Position is determined by the first finger and refers to the notes that can be covered by the normal finger placement without moving the hand. When your first finger is at the first fret, you can reach all the notes as far as the 4th fret. This is **first position**. If you move your first finger to the second fret (second position), you can include fifth fret notes within your normal reach. With the first finger at the third fret (third position), you can reach the 6th fret, and so on.

In second position, the new notes at the fifth fret are as shown below (numbers in circles are the string numbers):

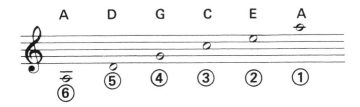

The second-position notes found at the 2nd, 3rd and 4th frets are already known to you. However, their fingering will be different. In the following exercises be sure to use the fingering given so that your hand stays in second position.

SECOND POSITION

The following melodies with their accompaniments are in a variety of contemporary music styles. Practice each melody carefully, using the fingering indicated. Some of the accompaniments have a rhythm that contrasts with that of the melody. Be sure to count accurately when playing the melody along with the record (try tapping your foot).

SECOND-POSITION ETUDE NO. 1

SECOND-POSITION ETUDE NO. 2

28

SECOND-POSITION ETUDE NO. 3

THE THIRD POSITION

The **third** position includes the new notes learned in the second position, plus the following notes at the 6th fret. (Notice the enharmonic pairs of notes on each string except the second.)

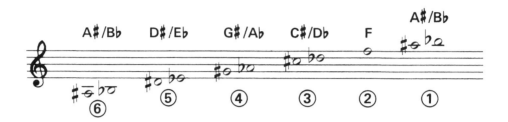

For now, concentrate on the treble string notes. Your notes in the following exercises will be on strings 1, 2 and 3.

THIRD-POSITION ETUDE NO. 1

THIRD-POSITION ETUDE NO. 2

COMBINING SECOND AND THIRD POSITIONS

JAZZ WALTZ uses both second and third positions. The shift to the third position (last measure of the second line) uses a **guide finger.** Guide fingers are indicated by dashes before numbers. You slide from one fret to the other with the guide finger. Relax the pressure of the finger but don't lift it off the string.

JAZZ WALTZ

32

GOD REST YE MERRY, GENTLEMEN uses a free alternation between second and third positions. It also includes repeated use of the note **G** on the 4th string. Observe the fingering indications carefully.

GOD REST YE MERRY, GENTLEMEN

THE KEY OF C MAJOR

Up until now, most of the music you've played has been in the keys of C and A minor. Occasionally you have played music written with a sharp or two as a key signature. From here on, new music will be introduced progressively by key signature, beginning with a review of the key of C.

The C scale has a characteristic pattern of half and whole steps. (W = whole and H = half.) The primary chords of the key are built on the 1st, 4th and 5th steps of the scale.

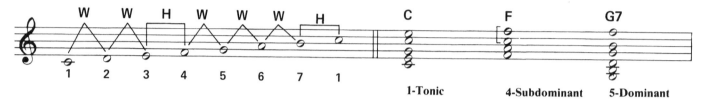

Fernando Sor (1778-1839) was the finest guitar composer of the early 19th century. In ANDANTE (which literally means a "walking" tempo), you should use the combination of rest- and free-strokes typical of this style of music. The first, second and third lines are mostly played with the free-stroke, since the character of the music is generally arpeggiated. (Notice also the occasional repetition of a finger in the interest of good finger to string correspondence.) The only notes that require the emphasis of rest-stroke are the long notes marked with an accent mark (>). In the fourth line the melody changes character—it moves by step, with the repeated rhythmic pattern of ♩ ♪ . Here, all the notes with stems up should be played with the rest-stroke.

ANDANTE

Sor

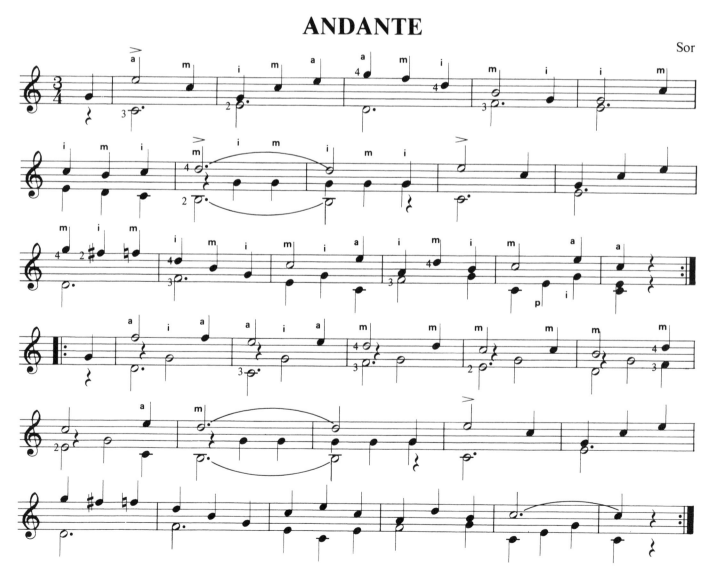

34

Melodies in the key of C often use a third-position fingering as in the following charming piece by Schumann. Use the **i-m** rest-stroke.

BAGATELLE

Robert Schumann

SIXTEENTH NOTES

Quarter notes may be subdivided into fourths to produce sixteenth notes. Sixteenth notes are written singly with two flags or together with a double beam:

A whole note may be subdivided evenly into smaller units as follows:

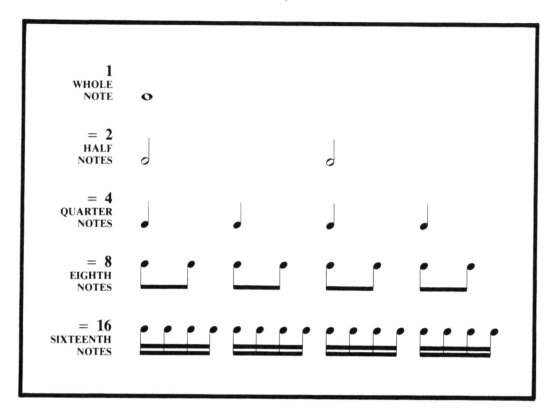

Sixteenth notes are counted by adding the syllable "a" (pronounced "uh") to the count:

Practice the following sixteenth note exercises using the **i-m** rest-stroke. Play in third position.

36

Notice below in the next to last measure the bracket fingering sign (1 [ ). This sign indicates a half bar, used here to play the notes G and D at the third fret with the first finger.

THIS OLD MAN

Play in 3rd position.

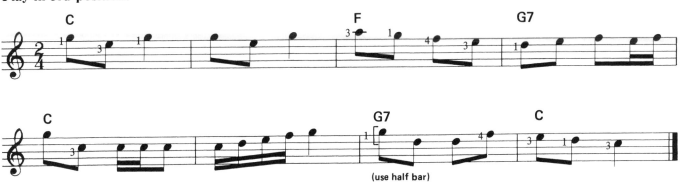

(use half bar)

Sixteenth notes are a way of subdividing the beat; they don't necessarily go fast. Play the following piece slowly, bringing out the melody carried by the **m** and **a** fingers.

PRELUDE IN C

Charles Duncan

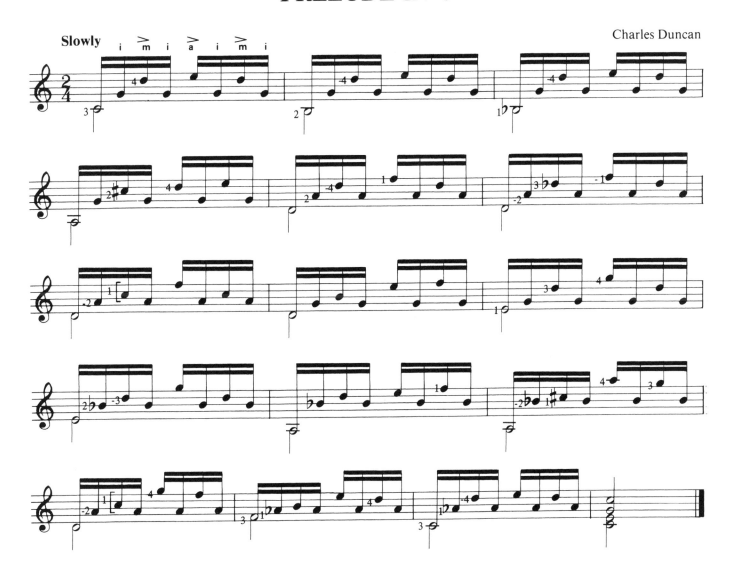

DOTTED EIGHTH NOTES

Like the other dotted notes you've played, the dot after an eighth note increases the value of the note by one-half.

Since the dotted eighth receives three-fourths of a beat in $\frac{4}{4}$, $\frac{3}{4}$ or $\frac{2}{4}$ time, a sixteenth is added to it to complete the beat.

A good way to learn a dotted eighth is to think of it as three tied sixteenth notes.

Once the dotted eighth-sixteenth figure is learned, the usual way to count is this:

THE BATTLE HYMN OF THE REPUBLIC

In the following piece by Mozart the dotted eighth is used as a **motive.**
(Motives are short musical ideas, usually a measure or less in length.) The
right-hand technique is the free-stroke with a modified alternation if **i** and **m.**
(Mofified alternation is often used to attain a more natural right-hand fingering.) Watch your left-hand fingering carefully in measures 2 and 3. The tempo
is leisurely, with a pulse only a little more than half of the BATTLE HYMN.

ANDANTE

W. A. Mozart

39

THE KEY OF A MINOR

The minor scale has a pattern of whole and half steps different from the major scale:

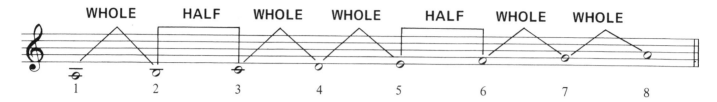

NATURAL MINOR SCALE

The above pattern is that of the **natural** minor. The minor scale has two other forms: **harmonic** and **melodic,** depending on chromatic differences in the sixth and seventh steps. Chords in the key of A minor are based on the harmonic minor scale. The harmonic minor has a sharped seventh degree.

HARMONIC MINOR SCALE

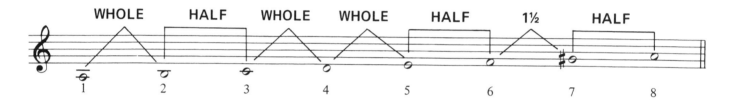

The melodic minor is the most commonly used form of the scale in melodies. In its ascending form, it has both the sixth and seventh degrees sharped.

MELODIC MINOR SCALE

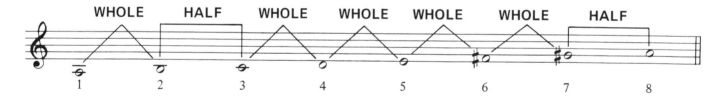

Descending, the sharps are omitted, so that in its descending form the melodic minor scale is the same as the natural minor.

Memorize and practice the following two-octave A melodic minor scale. In the second measure, notice that the scale goes temporarily into the second position. The return to the first position is accomplished by the 4th finger, which guides down from the 5th to the 3rd fret. Practice this scale with both **m-i** and **a-m** (rest-stroke). Practicing scales with **a-m** is an excellent way to strengthen the **a** finger.

You have already learned the primary chords in A minor. Once again, for review, they are Am, Dm and E:

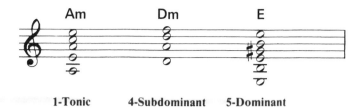

1-Tonic   4-Subdominant   5-Dominant

The following piece by Dionisio Aguado (1784-1849) is probably the best known study for the **p-i-m-i** arpeggio. (It has been recorded by Andres Segovia.) Aguado was a leading guitarist and teacher of the early 19th century.

The down-stems on the notes played by the thumb indicate they are to be held down while the other notes of the arpeggio are played. When the piece is played up to speed, the notes played by the thumb will be heard as a melody.

ESTUDIO IN Am

Aguado

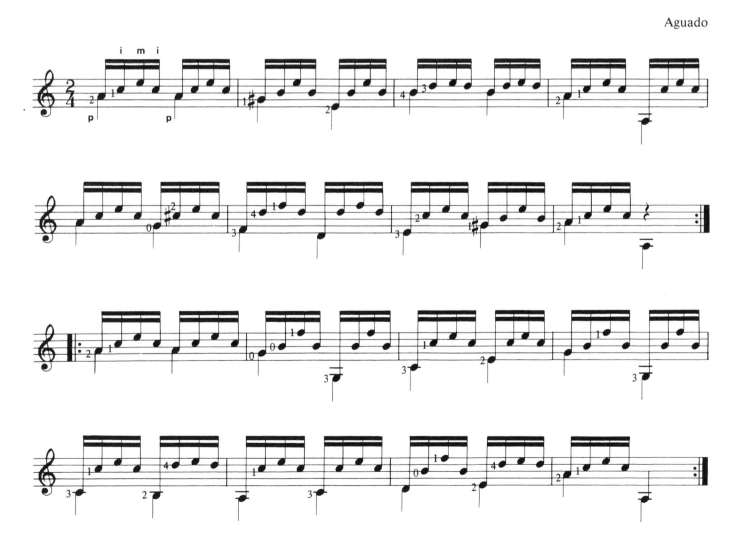

Gaspar Sanz (d. 1710) lived in late 17th century Spain. ESPAÑOLETA is a type of ancient Spanish dance in a graceful $\frac{3}{4}$ tempo. This piece, along with several others by Sanz, was used by the modern Spanish composer Joaquin Rodrigo as the basis of the beautiful guitar concerto FANTASIA PARA UN GENTILHOMBRE.

ESPAÑOLETA

Sanz

The following study in thirds by Carulli should be played at a gently rocking, lyrical tempo. The piece contains a frequently repeated left-hand challenge in the stretch of the 3rd and 4th fingers. Hold down the 1st finger as indicated by the dotted line for the first time this fingering occurs.

MODERATO

Carulli

PEZZO TEDESCO (meaning a German dance) comes from a 16th-century Italian lute manuscript. It is an extremely attractive piece in characteristic Renaissance style. (In music history, the Renaissance period extends from about 1475 to 1600)

You should spend some extra time mastering the unusual spacing of right-hand fingers in measure 3 before playing the entire piece.

PEZZO TEDESCO

Anonymous
16th Century

44

Leopold Mozart (1719-1787) was Wolfgang Amadeus Mozart's father and a composer in his own right. ENTREE is a type of dance from the Baroque period (approximately 1600-1750). It is in a fairly brisk 4/4 tempo.

The piece is constructed of two interdependent parts or voices, a treble and a bass melody. Play the bass and treble lines separately and notice that each has its own melodic integrity. When they are played together they form what is called **counterpoint**. Contrapuntal pieces on the guitar generally call for a lot of left-hand finger activity. Observe fingering indications carefully.

ENTRÉE

Leopold Mozart

SLURS

Notes played on the same string by the left hand alone are called **slurs**. They are indicated by the same kind of curved line that is used for **tied** notes. A tie connects two notes on the same pitch. In the case of slurs, the second note is different.

The technique of slurs depends on whether they are ascending or descending. The technique of ascending slurs is called **hammering-on**. The right hand plays a note; then, the appropriate left-hand finger falls on the next note like a hammer:

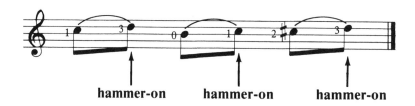

The attack of the hammered finger must be very forceful, with the tip of the finger absolutely rigid. (Think of your fingertip as a horse's hoof pounding onto the string!) The rhythm of slurs should be **even**. (There is a common tendency to rush the second note.) A good test is to play the same passage with slurs and without. The rhythm should be identical.

Practice ascending slurs in the following pattern:

The technique of descending slurs is called **pulling-off**. For descending slurs, the second note must be **already in place** when the first note is played. The left-hand finger plays the second note by flexing energetically from the tip-joint toward the palm, sounding the second note.

Now try the following descending slurs on the 1st string (all in 2nd position):

When the 2nd string is involved, descending slurs require more care. You must execute the second note cleanly without inadvertently sounding the first string. The best way to accomplish this is by treating the pull-off as a left-hand rest-stroke. Bring the slurring finger momentarily to rest against the first string as you pull-off. Try this procedure on the following second string slurs:

Now combine the various slurs you have practiced in the following exercise. Remember, the rhythm should be just as even as if you played each note with the right hand.

If you can play the previous exercise, you should have no trouble playing the melody in the following duet adapted from a harpsichord piece by Jean Philippe Rameau, a French composer of the 18th century. The mixture of slurs with plucked notes is typical of much classical guitar music.

RONDINO

Rameau

MUSIC THEORY REVIEW

1. Write in the number of the fret for the following second- and third-position notes:

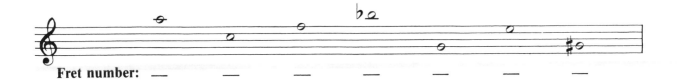

Fret number: ___   ___   ___   ___   ___   ___   ___

2. Write in the correct left-hand fingering for the following third-position scale pattern:

Finger: ___   ___   ___   ___   ___   ___   ___   ___   ___   ___   ___   ___

3. Write in the missing sharps necessary to make the following into an ascending A melodic minor scale:

4. There are two half-steps in the C major scale. They are between the letters _____ and _____ , and between _____ and _____ .

5. A short musical idea usually consisting of a measure or less is called a _____ .

6. The interdependent movement of two parts (or voices), each with its own melodic integrity, is known as _____ .

7. The names of the primary chords built on steps 1, 4, and 5 of any scale are _____ , _____ , and _____ (7th).

THE PHRYGIAN MODE

Music that sounds typically Spanish is often in the **Phrygian mode.** The Phrygian mode is a scale pattern of half and whole steps that results when you begin and end a scale on E without any sharps or flats.

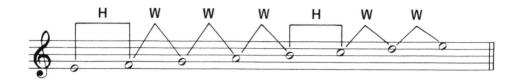

The chords built on steps 1, 2, 3, and 4 serve as primary chords for Spanish music in the Phrygian mode. In E, they are chords you already know: E, F, G, and Am. Usually they occur in reverse order in the harmonization of Spanish music—Am-G-F-E. (Other common chord sequences would include E-F-E, F-G-F-E, etc.) Here are some typical Phrygian melodic patterns. The note G♯ occasionally occurs when the melody implies an E chord.

The famous melody of MALAGUEÑA (pronounced mah-lah-gain-ya) is based on the Phrygian mode. The melody is a traditional flamenco guitar pattern from the city of Malaga.

MALAGUEÑA

When the Phrygian mode is built on any note other than E, chromatic alterations must be used to keep the same half-step/whole-step arrangement. FIESTA is based on an A Phrygian mode, which uses a B♭ plus occasional C♯s.

FIESTA

Charles Duncan

THE KEY OF G MAJOR

The G major scale has the same pattern of whole and half steps as the C major scale you studied. The seventh degree of the scale (F) must be sharped to create the whole-step between 6 and 7 and the half-step between 7 and 1. A key signature of one sharp is used for all pieces in G major.

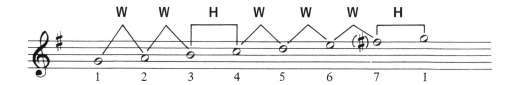

Memorize and practice the following two-octave G major scale. Use the **m-i** and **a-m** rest-stroke. (Be sure to practice with **m-a**. This will help to strengthen the **a** finger and improve the balance of touch throughout the hand.)

The primary chords in the key of G major are G, C, and D7. Notice that there are two standard fingerings for the G chord. Eventually you should be able to use either of them. For now, you may prefer to use the first fingering.

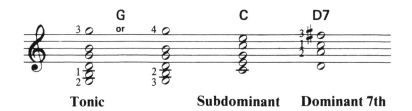

Practice the chords in the following exercise; then play the arpeggiated accompaniment to SILENT NIGHT.

Use Thumb Brush

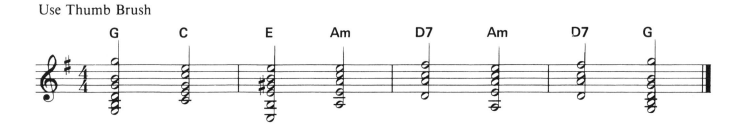

52

SILENT NIGHT

Franz Gruber

The following well-known minuet by Bach is based on G major scale patterns.
Slurs are used systematically to enhance the rhythmic drive of each group of
eighth notes.

MINUET IN G

J. S. Bach

This equally famous minuet by Beethoven has a more complex rhythm and is played in a slower tempo. Notice the change from dotted notes to straight eighths near the end of the first period, and the group of sixteenth notes in measure two of the third staff.

MINUET IN G

Ludwig van Beethoven

The following solos by Carulli and Sor begin with nearly identical melodic statements; however, they develop differently and are quite different in character. This is a good illustration of how much musical variety is possible even when the compositional material is very similar. Of the two, the Sor has a somewhat more challenging left-hand technique. Notice especially the overlapping note values and the use of second and third positions.

MODERATO

Carulli

ANDANTINO

Sor

56

The following is another attractive example of Renaissance music style. Fabritio Caroso was an Italian lutenist of the 16th century. A collection of his music which includes this courtly dance was published in Venice in 1581. The right-hand technique is generally **i-m** alternation using the free-stroke.

GRATIA D'AMORE

Caroso

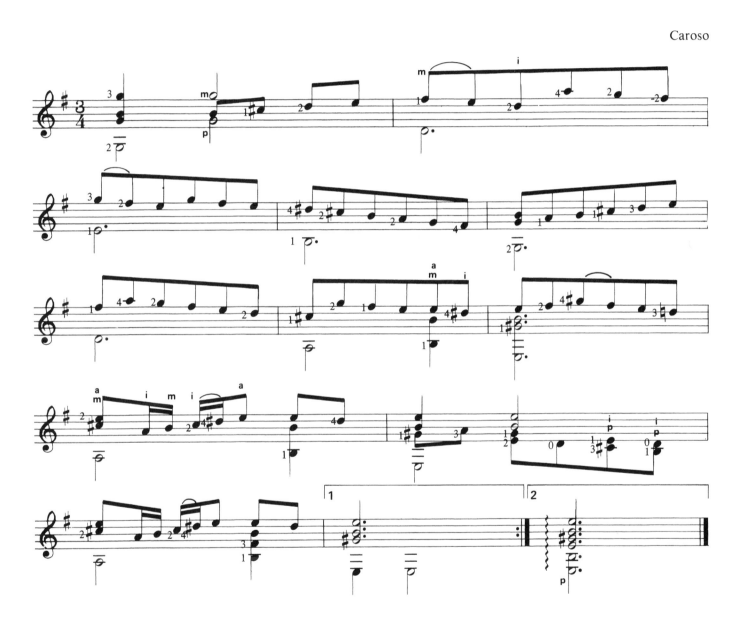

THE KEY OF E MINOR

Major and minor keys that have the same key signature are relatives. The relative minor of C is Am; the relative minor of G is Em.

The relative minor scale in its natural form begins on the sixth degree of the major scale with the same key signature.

TWO-OCTAVE G SCALE

E minor scale

Memorize and practice the two-octave E melodic minor scale.

The primary chords for E minor are Em, Am, and B7. The new chord is B7: You can learn to shift to and from it much more efficiently if you practice leaving down a finger where possible. From Em to B7, leave down 2; from Am to B7, leave down 3.

Now practice the following chord changes:

To practice your chord changes in Em, play the accompaniment to this fine old English ballad. The G and D7 chords are also used, because the melody passes freely from E minor to G major harmonizations.

HENRY MARTIN

The following is another piece from Fabritio Caroso's book of lute music. Although written in E minor, the dominant-to-tonic resolution at the end of the first, third, and fourth lines involves an E major chord. The device of ending on a major chord in a minor key is called a **Picardy third** and is characteristic of much Renaissance music. Play the piece with an energetic, steady beat as if accompanying a dance.

ALBA NOVELLA

Caroso

REMEMBRANCE is in a Romantic style—that is, the 19th-century style typified by composers such as Schubert, Schumann, and Mendelssohn. The melody should be emphasized with feeling by using the rest-stroke wherever convenient. When you must use the free-stroke on melody notes, try to make them stand out.

REMEMBRANCE

Charles Duncan

For further practice in position playing, here is one of the most majestic short works by Bach. Play the melody entirely in second position with very solid rest-strokes. The essential feeling should be one of solemnity and grandeur.

"Chorale" from the ST. MATTHEW PASSION

J. S. Bach

To conclude this volume, here is one of Sor's prettiest compositions. In measure 2, the small note **D** at the beginning is a **grace note**. Grace notes are a form of **ornamentation** or **embellishment** and should be played in this piece as shown below:

You play the grace note **together** with any notes below the note to which the grace note is slurred. Then you pull-off to the slurred note as rapidly as possible. The procedure may sound complicated, but it isn't really. Listen closely to the recording for illustration.

ANDANTE

Sor

CLASSICAL GUITAR PUBLICATIONS FROM HAL LEONARD

THE BEATLES FOR CLASSICAL GUITAR

Includes 20 solos from big Beatles hits arranged for classical guitar, complete with left-hand and right-hand fingering. Songs include: All My Loving • And I Love Her • Can't Buy Me Love • Fool on the Hill • From a Window • Hey Jude • If I Fell • Let It Be • Michelle • Norwegian Wood • Obla Di • Ticket to Ride • Yesterday • and more. Features arrangements and an introduction by Joe Washington, as well as his helpful hints on classical technique and detailed notes on how to play each song. The book also covers parts and specifications of the classical guitar, tuning, and Joe's "Strata System" – an easy-reading system applied to chord diagrams.

_____00699237 Classical Guitar $17.99

MATTEO CARCASSI – 25 MELODIC AND PROGRESSIVE STUDIES, OP. 60 • *arr. Paul Henry*

One of Carcassi's (1792-1853) most famous collections of classical guitar music – indispensable for the modern guitarist's musical and technical development. Performed by Paul Henry. 49-minute audio accompaniment.

_____00696506 Book/CD Pack $17.95

CLASSICAL & FINGERSTYLE GUITAR TECHNIQUES

by David Oakes • Musicians Institute

This Master Class with MI instructor David Oakes is aimed at any electric or acoustic guitarist who wants a quick, thorough grounding in the essentials of classical and fingerstyle technique. Topics covered include: arpeggios and scales, free stroke and rest stroke, P-i scale technique, three-to-a-string patterns, natural and artificial harmonics, tremolo and rasgueado, and more. The book includes 12 intensive lessons for right and left hand in standard notation & tab, and the CD features 92 solo acoustic tracks.

_____00695171 Book/CD Pack $16.95

CLASSICAL GUITAR CHRISTMAS COLLECTION

Includes classical guitar arrangements in standard notation and tablature for more than two dozen beloved carols: Angels We Have Heard on High • Auld Lang Syne • Ave Maria • Away in a Manger • Canon in D • The First Noel • God Rest Ye Merry, Gentlemen • Hark! the Herald Angels Sing • I Saw Three Ships • Jesu, Joy of Man's Desiring • Joy to the World • O Christmas Tree • O Holy Night • Silent Night • What Child Is This? • and more.

_____00699493 Guitar Solo $9.95

CLASSICAL MASTERPIECES FOR GUITAR

27 works by Bach, Beethoven, Handel, Mendelssohn, Mozart and more transcribed with standard notation and tablature. Now anyone can enjoy classical material regardless of their guitar background. Also features stay-open binding.

_____00699312 ....$12.95

FOR MORE INFORMATION, SEE YOUR LOCAL MUSIC DEALER,
OR WRITE TO:

HAL•LEONARD® CORPORATION

7777 W. BLUEMOUND RD. P.O. BOX 13819 MILWAUKEE, WI 53213

Visit Hal Leonard Online at **www.halleonard.com**

Prices, contents and availability subject to change without notice.

CLASSICAL THEMES

20 beloved classical themes arranged for easy guitar in large-size notes (with the note names in the note heads) and tablature. Includes: Air on the G String (Bach) • Ave Maria (Schubert) • Für Elise (Beethoven) • In the Hall of the Mountain King (Grieg) • Jesu, Joy of Man's Desiring (Bach) • Largo (Handel) • Ode to Joy (Beethoven) • Pomp and Circumstance (Elgar) • and more. Ideal for beginning or vision-impaired players.

_____00699272 E-Z Play Guitar $9.95

MASTERWORKS FOR GUITAR

Over 60 Favorites from Four Centuries • World's Great Classical Music

Dozens of classical masterpieces: Allemande • Bourree • Canon in D • Jesu, Joy of Man's Desiring • Lagrima • Malaguena • Mazurka • Piano Sonata No. 14 in C# Minor (Moonlight) Op. 27 No. 2 First Movement Theme • Ode to Joy • Prelude No. I (Well-Tempered Clavier).

_____00699503 ....$16.95

A MODERN APPROACH TO CLASSICAL GUITAR • *by Charles Duncan*

This multi-volume method was developed to allow students to study the art of classical guitar within a new, more contemporary framework. For private, class or self-instruction. Book One incorporates chord frames and symbols, as well as a recording to assist in tuning and to provide accompaniments for at-home practice. Book One also introduces beginning fingerboard technique and music theory. Book Two and Three build upon the techniques learned in Book One.

_____00695114 Book 1 – Book Only..$6.99
_____00695113 Book 1 – Book/CD Pack..$10.95
_____00695116 Book 2 – Book Only..$6.95
_____00695115 Book 2 – Book/CD Pack..$10.95
_____00699202 Book 3 – Book Only..$7.95
_____00695117 Book 3 – Book/CD Pack..$10.95
_____00695119 Composite Book/CD Pack.......................................$27.95

ANDRES SEGOVIA – 20 STUDIES FOR GUITAR • *Sor/Segovia*

20 studies for the classical guitar written by Beethoven's contemporary, Fernando Sor, revised, edited and fingered by the great classical guitarist Andres Segovia. These essential repertoire pieces continue to be used by teachers and students to build solid classical technique. Features a 50-minute demonstration CD.

_____00695012 Book/CD Pack $18.95
_____00006363 Book Only...$7.95

THE FRANCISCO TÁRREGA COLLECTION

edited and performed by Paul Henry

Considered the father of modern classical guitar, Francisco Tárrega revolutionized guitar technique and composed a wealth of music that will be a cornerstone of classical guitar repertoire for centuries to come. This unique book/CD pack features 14 of his most outstanding pieces in standard notation and tab, edited and performed on CD by virtuoso Paul Henry. Includes: Adelita • Capricho Árabe • Estudio Brillante • Grand Jota • Lágrima • Malagueña • María • Recuerdos de la Alhambra • Tango • and more, plus bios of Tárrega and Henry.

_____00698993 Book/CD Pack $19.99

0809